FC Barc

Quiz Book

101 Questions That Will Test Your Knowledge
Of The Most Successful Football Club In Spain

Published by Glowworm Press
7 Nuffield Way
Abingdon OX14 1RL
By Chris Carpenter

Barcelona Football Club

This book contains one hundred and one informative
and entertaining trivia questions with multiple choice
answers. With 101 questions, some easy, some more
demanding, this entertaining book will really test your
knowledge of Barcelona Football Club.

You will be quizzed on a wide range of topics associated
with Barcelona football club for you to test yourself;
with questions on players, managers, opponents,
transfer deals, trophies, records, fixtures and more,
guaranteeing you a truly educational experience. The
FC Barcelona Quiz Book will provide entertainment for
fans of all ages, and will certainly test your knowledge
of this world famous club. The book is packed with
information and is a must-have for Barcelona
supporters wherever you live in the world.

2019-20 Season Edition

FOREWORD

When I was asked to write a foreword to this book I was very flattered.

I have known the author Chris Carpenter for a number of years and his knowledge of facts and figures is incredible.

His love for football and his skill in writing quiz books make him the ideal man to pay homage to my great love Barcelona Football Club.

This book came about as a result of a challenge on a golf course.

I do hope you enjoy the book.

Javier Costa

Let's start with some relatively easy questions.

1. When was Barcelona founded?
   - A. 1897
   - B. 1898
   - C. 1899

2. What is Barcelona's nickname?
   - A. Blaubueno
   - B. Blaugrana
   - C. Guarana

3. What is the motto of FC Barcelona?
   - A. Most famous club
   - B. More than a club
   - C. More to life

4. Where does Barcelona play their home games?
   - A. Camp Nou
   - B. Mestalla Stadium
   - C. El Prat

5. What is the stadium's capacity?
   - A. 97,435
   - B. 98,543
   - C. 99,354

6. What is the club's training academy called?
   - A. La Basia
   - B. La Dasia
   - C. La Masia

7. Who has made the most appearances for the club in total?
   A. Andres Iniesta
   B. Carles Puyol
   C. Xavi

8. Who has made the most *League* appearances for the club?
   A. Andres Iniesta
   B. Migueli
   C. Xavi

9. Who is the club's record goal scorer?
   A. Cesar Alvarez
   B. Laszlo Kubala
   C. Lionel Messi

10. Who or what is the club mascot?
   A. L'Avi del Barça
   B. El Cid
   C. El Loco

OK, so here are the answers to the first ten questions. If you get seven or more right, you are doing very well so far, but the questions do get harder.

A1. Barcelona was founded on 29th November 1899, as Foot-Ball Club Barcelona.

A2. Barcelona's nickname is Blaugrana, in reference to the team colours in the Catalan language. In Catalan, blau means blue and gran translates to deep red.

A3. FC Barcelona is a symbol of Catalan culture and Catalanism, hence the motto "Mes que un club" ("More than a club").

A4. Barcelona plays their home games at the Camp Nou Stadium.

A5. The Camp Nou stadium's capacity is currently 99,354 making it the largest football stadium in Spain and in Europe, and the third largest football stadium in the world.

A6. La Masia de Can Planes, usually shortened to La Masia (in English "The Farmhouse") is the club's youth academy.

A7. Xavi (Xavier Hernandez) holds the record for the most appearances in all competitions, with a grand total of 769. Legend.

A8. Xavi has also made the most league appearances, with a total of 505 games. Xavi is actually a son of a former professional soccer player and he demonstrated impressive athletic abilities at an early age and joined La Masia at the age of 11.

A9. Unsurprisingly Lionel Messi is Barcelona's all-time top scorer. He has scored over 600 goals in all competitions for the club. The Argentine could also manage to grasp the record for most La Liga victories, as he is a few games away from matching the 334 of Real Madrid's former goalkeeper Iker Casillas.

A10. FC Barcelona's mascot is a human being. "L'Avi del Barça" is an elderly man with a beard. It translates as "The Grandfather of Barcelona" in the Catalan language.

OK, back to the questions.

11. What is the highest number of goals that FC Barcelona has scored in a league season?
    A. 115
    B. 116
    C. 117

12. What is the fewest number of goals that the club has conceded in a league season?
    A. 32
    B. 34
    C. 36

13. What is the record number of goals the club has scored in a season in all competitions?
    A. 170
    B. 180
    C. 190

14. What is the record attendance at the Camp Nou for a football match?
    A. 100,000
    B. 110,000
    C. 120,000

15. Where did FC Barcelona originally play their home games?
    A. Camp de Les Corts
    B. Camp de la Industria
    C. Camp de la Revolucion

16. When did Barcelona move to Camp Nou stadium?
    A. 1955
    B. 1956
    C. 1957

17. What is the size of the pitch?
    A. 104x67m
    B. 105x68m
    C. 106x69m

18. What is the name of the road the ground is on?
    A. Aristides Maillol
    B. Carrer de Badal
    C. Ronda del Litoral

19. What is FC Barcelona's training ground called?
    A. Ciudad Esportiva Joan Gamper
    B. Ciudad de Stefano
    C. Valdebebas

20. What match was played at the stadium on 24th May 1972?
    A. Champions League Final
    B. European Cup Winners' Cup Final
    C. UEFA Cup Final

Here are the answers to the last set of questions.

A11. Barcelona scored a record total of 116 goals in 38 matches in the 2016-17 season.

A12. Barcelona scored the least number of 32 goals in 22 games during the 1939-40 season.

A13. By scoring 180 goals in 2015 in all competitions, Barcelona set the record for most goals scored in a calendar year, breaking Real Madrid's record of 178 goals scored in 2014.

A14. Barcelona played Juventus in a European game on 5th March 1986 in front of 120,000 people; back when standing was allowed at the stadium.

A15. Barcelona initially played in the Camp de la Industria which was a multi-use stadium with a capacity of 6,000. How times have changed!

A16. Camp Nou was built between 1954 and 1957, and officially opened on the 24th September 1957. The first played match was between FC Barcelona and a selection of players from the city of Warsaw.

A17. The playing area is 105 metres long and 68 metres wide, in accordance with UEFA stipulations.

A18. The ground is located on Aristides Maillol.

A19. The Ciutat Esportiva Joan Gamper is the training ground. It was officially opened on 1st June 2006 and was named in honour of Joan Gamper, the founder of the club.

A20. On 24th May1972 Camp Nou hosted the European Cup Winners' Cup Final between Rangers and Dynamo Moscow, which Rangers won 3-2.

Now we move onto some questions about the club's records.

21. What is the club's highest win in European competition at away games?
    A. 6-1
    B. 7-0
    C. 7-3

22. Who did they beat?
    A. Hapoel Tel Aviv
    B. Hapoel Haifa
    C. Hapoel Be'er Sheva

23. In which season?
    A. 1991-92
    B. 1993-94
    C. 1995-96

24. What is the club's record home win in La Liga?
    A. 10-0
    B. 10-1
    C. 10-2

25. Who did they beat?
    A. Atletico Madrid
    B. Gimnastic de Tarragona
    C. Huesca

26. In which season?
    A. 1949-50

B. 1959-60
C. 1969-70

27. What is the club's record defeat?
 A. 1-9
 B. 1-10
 C. 1-11

28. Who has scored the most hat tricks in La Liga for Barcelona?
 A. Diego Maradona
 B. Lionel Messi
 C. Hristo Stoichkov

29. Who has scored the most goals in a La Liga season?
 A. Lionel Messi
 B. Ronaldinho
 C. Luis Suarez

30. What is the record number of points the club has ever achieved in a season?
 A. 96
 B. 98
 C. 100

Here are the answers to the last set of questions.

A21. The club's highest win in European competition at away games is 7-0.

A22. The club beat Hapoel Be'er Sheva from Israel.

A23. The match took place on 12th of September 1995, in a European Cup match during the 1995-96 season.

A24. The club's record win in La Liga is 10-1.

A25. Barcelona trashed Gimnastic de Tarragona.

A26. Barcelona marked the biggest league home win in their history on 10th September 1949, so it was during the 1949-50 season.

A27. The club's record defeat in any competition is 11-1, when the club lost to Real Madrid on the 13th June 1943, in the second leg of a semi-final of the Copa del Generalisimo (Copa del Rey).

A28. Messi has scored 33 La Liga hat tricks for the club before the start of the 2019-20 season. It is an incredible achievement. Cristiano Ronaldo scored a record 34 hat tricks in La Liga, so this record should be broken by Messi this season.

A29. It's that man Lionel Messi again. He holds the record for most goals scored in a season with 50 goals in 2011-12.

A30. With Pep Guardiola as manager, the club amassed 100 points during the 2012-13 season.

Now we move onto some questions about the club's trophies.

31. How many times have Barcelona won La Liga?
    A. 30
    B. 33
    C. 36

32. How many times have Barcelona won the Copa del Rey?
    A. 24
    B. 27
    C. 30

33. How many times have Barcelona won the Supercopa de Espana?
    A. 12
    B. 13
    C. 14

34. When did the club win their first La Liga title?
    A. 1926-27
    B. 1927-28
    C. 1928-29

35. When did the club win their first Copa Del Rey?
    A. 1910
    B. 1920
    C. 1930

36. When did the club win their first Supercopa de Espana?
    A. 1981
    B. 1983
    C. 1985

37. How many times has Barcelona won the league and Cup double?
    A. 6
    B. 7
    C. 8

38. When was the last time Barcelona won the league and Cup double?
    A. 2015-16
    B. 2016-17
    C. 2017-18

39. Who was the captain of FC Barcelona when they won their first treble (League, Cup and Champions League)?
    A. Andres Iniesta
    B. Carles Puyol
    C. Jose Manuel Pinto

40. How many Barcelona players have won the World Player of the Year award?
    A. 5
    B. 6
    C. 7

Here are the answers to the last block of questions.

A31. Barcelona has won the La Liga championship 36 times

A32. Barcelona has won the Copa Del Rey (in English, the King's Cup) a record 30 times, most recently in 2018.

A33. The Supercopa de Espana is contested between the winners of La Liga and the Copa Del Rey of the previous season. Barcelona has won the Supercopa de Espana a record 13 times, most recently in 2018.

A34. Barcelona won their first La Liga title at the end of the 1928-29 season.

A35. Barcelona won their first Copa Del Rey in 1910.

A36. The first time Barcelona won the Supercopa de Espana was in 1983.

A37. Barcelona has won a record 8 doubles of La Liga and Copa del Rey in the same season.

A38. The last time Barcelona won the domestic double was 2017-18.

A39. Barcelona has won the treble (La Liga, Copa del Rey and Champions League) in the same season twice –

in 2008-09 and 2014-15. Carles Puyol was the captain of the team when Barcelona won their first treble.

A40. Five Barcelona players have won the FIFA World Player of the Year award – four Brazilians and one Argentinian. They are Romario, Ronaldo, Rivaldo, Ronaldinho and of course Messi.

I hope you're having fun, and getting most of the answers right.

41. Who was the first manager of the club?
    A. Joan Gumper
    B. Ramon Llorens
    C. Alf Spouncer

42. Who is the club's longest serving manager of all time?
    A. Pep Guardiola
    B. Joan Gumper
    C. Helenio Herrera

43. Who is considered the club's most successful manager of all time?
    A. Luis Enrique
    B. Pep Guardiola
    C. Ernesto Valverde

44. Which of these men won the FIFA Club World Cup whilst manager at the club?
    A. Radomir Antic
    B. Luis Enrique
    C. Carles Rexach

45. How many English managers has the club had?
    A. 5
    B. 7
    C. 9

46. Which ex manager went on to manage the national team?
    A. Luis Enrique
    B. Pep Guardiola
    C. Ernesto Valverde

47. Who started the 2018-19 season as manager?
    A. Luis Enrique
    B. Gerardo Martino
    C. Ernesto Valverde

48. Who was the captain when the club won the 2006 Champions League?
    A. Samuel Eto'o
    B. Luis Figo
    C. Carles Puyol

49. Who is the longest – serving captain in FC Barcelona's history?
    A. Carles Puyol
    B. Jose Ramon Alexanko
    C. Antoni Torres

50. Who started the 2019-20 season as club captain?
    A. Jordi Alba
    B. Sergio Busquets
    C. Lionel Messi

Here are the answers to the last set of questions.

A41. The first manager of FC Barcelona was Joan Gamper from Switzerland. He managed the team from 1902 to 1917.

A42. Joan Gumper is also the club's longest serving manager of all time. He managed the club into winning 3 Copa del Rey, 1 Copa Macaya, 1 Copa Barcelona and 7 Campionat de Catalanuya titles.

A43. FC Barcelona won a whopping 14 trophies in just 4 seasons with Guardiola as their team manager. From June 2008 to June 2012, Barça won 3 La Liga, 2 Copa del Rey, 3 Supercopa de Espana, 2 Champions League, 2 UEFA Super cup and 2 FIFA Club World Cup trophies.

A44. Luis Enrique managed FC Barcelona from May 2014 to May 2017. He led the team to 1 FIFA Club World Cup, 2 La Liga, 3 Copa del Rey, 1 Supercopa de Espana, 1 Champions League and 1 UEFA Super Cup title.

A45. FC Barcelona has had 9 English managers. They are John Barrow (1917), Jack Greenwell (1917 to 1923), Alf Spouncer (1923 to 1924), Ralph Kirby (1924 to 1926), James Bellamy (1929 to 1931), Jack Greenwell (1931 to 1933), Vic Buckingham (1969 to 1971), Terry Venables (1984 to 1987) and Bobby Robson (1996 to 1997).

A46. Luis Enrique was appointed as Spain's coach on 9th July 2018.

A47. Ernesto Valverde started the 2018-19 season as the manager. He became the manager of the club in May 2017.

A48. On 17th May 2006 in Stade de France in Paris, Carles Puyol lifted the 2006 Champions League trophy after Barcleona had beaten Arsenal 2-1 in the final.

A49. Carles Puyol is the man who carries the title for longest serving captain in the history of FC Barcelona.

A50. Starting from 2018, Lionel Messi carries the title of the captain of the team after he took over the role following the departure of Andrés Iniesta.

I hope you're learning some new facts about the club, and here is the next set of questions.

51. What is the record transfer fee paid?
    A. €135 million
    B. €140 million
    C. €145 million

52. Who was the record transfer fee paid for?
    A. Philippe Coutinho
    B. Neymar
    C. Luis Suarez

53. What is the record transfer fee received?
    A. €206 million
    B. €214 million
    C. €222 million

54. Who was the record transfer fee received for?
    A. Ousmane Dembele
    B. Neymar
    C. Arturo Vidal

55. What nationality is Luis Suarez?
    A. Brazilian
    B. Colombian
    C. Uruguayan

56. What shirt number does Antoine Griezmann wear?
    A. 7

B. 11

C. 17

57. What is the nickname of Gerard Pique?
    A. Piquenbauer
    B. Rocket
    C. The Illusionist

58. Who is the player who has scored the most goals in one league match for the club?
    A. Laszlo Kubala
    B. Lionel Messi
    C. Luis Suarez

59. What position did the club finish at the end of the 2018-19 season?
    A. 1st
    B. 2nd
    C. 3rd

60. Who is the youngest player to ever appear for Barcelona?
    A. Paulino Alcantara
    B. Bojan Krkic
    C. Vicente Martinez

Here are the answers to the last set of questions.

A51. In January 2018 Barcelona paid €135 million for a Brazilian midfielder.

A52. Barcelona's record transfer fee paid out was for Philippe Coutinho who moved from Liverpool.

A53. In August 2017 Barcelona received €222 million from Paris Saint-Germain.

A54. Barcelona's record transfer fee received was for Brazilian attacker Neymar.

A55. Luis Alberto Suárez Díaz is Uruguayan.

A56. Antoine Griezmann wears the number 17 shirt. Philippe Coutinho wears the number 7 shirt.

A57. Gerard Pique carries the nickname Piquenbauer, a combination of Piqué's name and former German footballer, Franz Beckenbauer.

A58. Laszlo Kubala scored a total of seven goals in one game for FC Barcelona. The game was held on the 10th February 1952 against Sporting Gijon and the match ended 9-0.

A59. Barcelona finished the 2018-19 season as champions. They finished with 87 points, 11 clear of second placed Atletico.

A60. Paulino Alcantara is the youngest player to appear for the club aged just 15 years, 4 months and 18 days. His debut was on 25th February 1912 against Catala SC in the Campionat de Catalunya, a game Barcelona won 9-0. Alcantara scored the first three goals of the game setting the still unbroken record for being the youngest player to ever score for Barcelona in an official match.

Let's give you some easier questions.

61. What is the traditional colour of the home shirt?
    A. Blue and garnet
    B. Blue and black
    C. Red and white

62. What is the present colour of the away shirt?
    A. Black
    B. Green
    C. Red

63. Who is the current club shirt sponsor?
    A. Qatar Airways
    B. Rakuten
    C. Siemens

64. Who was the first club shirt sponsor?
    A. Kappa
    B. Lacoste
    C. Meyba

65. Which organization cooperates closely with the Foundation of FC Barcelona?
    A. International Red Cross
    B. Unicef
    C. World Food Programme

66. Who currently supplies kit to the club?
    A. Adidas
    B. Converse

C. Nike

67. Which of these has never sponsored the club?
    A. Nike
    B. Qatar Airways
    C. Under Armour

68. What motif is on top of the club crest?
    A. Cross
    B. Crown
    C. Flag

69. What colours are in the stripe on the club badge?
    A. Blue and maroon
    B. Red and black
    C. Red and yellow

70. What are the club's supporters called?
    A. Barcelonistas
    B. Culés
    C. Matadors

Here are the answers to the last ten questions.

A61. The traditional colour of the home shirt is of course blue and garnet.

A62. The present away kit of FC Barcelona comes in a luminous lime green called Volt.

A63. Prior to the 2017-18 season, the club signed a four year deal with the Japanese electronic commerce and internet company Rakuten. The name now appears in the middle of the chest in white letters.

A64. In the period from 1899 to 1982, Barcelona did not have any supplier. In the period from 1982 to 1992 Barcelona received sponsorship by Meyba.

A65. The Foundation of FC Barcelona and Unicef are in close mutual cooperation and are active philanthropically. The club currently donates approximately €2 million each year to the charity.

A66. The main partner of FC Barcelona for their supplying kit is Nike. This is a long term cooperation that started in 1998.

A67. Under Armour has never been a sponsor of the club; whereas Nike and Qatar Airways have.

A68. The top quarters contain the St. George's Cross, representing the patron saint of Catalonia and which is also present in the coat of arms of the city of Barcelona, and the Catalan flag. The bottom quarters contain the colours of the Club and a ball, which is central to the crest and the Barcelona style of play.

A69. The flag of Barcelona combines the cross of Saint George (in Catalan, Sant Jordi), the patron saint of Catalonia, with the traditional red and yellow bars of the Senyera, the ancient symbol of the Crown of Aragon.

A70. FC Barcelona supporters are called culés and the word means "ass" in Catalan. According to the legend, during the twenties in the former Stadium in Les Corts, passer-bys could see the bums of supporters sat in the highest row of the stadium.

Here are some questions about the club's achievements in European football.

71. How many times have Barcelona won the European Cup / Champions League?
    A. 4
    B. 5
    C. 6

72. Who was the club's first European Cup final victory against?
    A. Arsenal
    B. Sampdoria
    C. Manchester United

73. Who was the manager of Barcelona when the team won their first European Cup?
    A. Johan Cruyff
    B. Carles Rexach
    C. Llorenc Serra Ferrer

74. Who was the club's last Champions League final victory against?
    A. Atletico Madrid
    B. Juventus
    C. Manchester United

75. Who did the club beat 4-3 in the 1979 UEFA Cup Final?
    A. Fortuna Dusseldorf
    B. Eintracht Frankfurt

C. Sampdoria

76. Who scored the most goals in one Championship League season?
    A. Samuel Eto'o
    B. Laszlo Kubala
    C. Lionel Messi

77. What is the record number of consecutive wins by the club in the Champions League?
    A. 7
    B. 9
    C. 11

78. In which season did Barcelona score 45 goals in the Champions League?
    A. 1998-1999
    B. 1999-2000
    C. 2000-2001

79. Who was the manager of the side that won the Champions League in 2006?
    A. Pep Guardiola
    B. Frank Rijkaard
    C. Tito Vitanova

80. Who was the manager of the side that won the Champions League in 2015?
    A. Pep Guardiola
    B. Luis Enrique
    C. Tito Vitanova

Here are the answers to the last set of questions.

A71. Barcelona has won the European Cup/Champions League trophy five times (in season 1991-92, 2005-06, 2008-09, 2010-11 and 2014-15).

A72. On 20th May 1992, Barcelona won their first European Cup/Champions League after beating Sampdoria 1-0 at Wembley Stadium in London. The goal was scored by Ronald Koeman.

A73. The manager who led the team to their first European Cup in 1992 was Johan Cruyff.

A74. On 6th June 2015 Barcelona beat Juventus 3-1 in the 2015 Champions League final in Berlin. The goals were scored by Rakitic, Suarez and Neymar.

A75. Barcelona won the UEFA Cup Winners' Cup beating Fortuna Dusseldorf 4-3 on 16th May 1979. This was the first of four occasions that the club has won the tournament.

A76. Lionel Messi scored 14 goals for Barcelona during one Champions League season in 2011-12.

A77. During the 2002-03 season Barcelona achieved 11 consecutive wins in the Champions League.

A78. In the 1999-2000 season Barcelona scored 45 goals in the Champions League.

A79. The Dutch manager Frank Rijkaard managed Barcelona to their 2006 Champions League victory. In the final on 17th May Barcelona beat Arsenal 2-1 at The Stade de France in Paris.

A80. Spanish manager Luis Enrique managed Barcelona to their 2015 Champions League victory, when they overcome Juventus 3-1 in the final.

Here are the next set of questions, let's hope you get most of them right.

81. What is the biggest win for Barcelona in any competition?
   A. 12-0
   B. 15-0
   C. 18-0

82. What is the longest unbeaten run in all competitive matches for Barcelona?
   A. 33
   B. 36
   C. 39

83. What is the highest number in victories that Barcelona made in a season?
   A. 40
   B. 45
   C. 50

84. What is the record number of goals Barcelona has scored in all competitions in one season?
   A. 170
   B. 180
   C. 190

85. Who was the first Barcelona goalkeeper to win the Zamora trophy?
   A. Antoni Ramallets
   B. Miguel Reina

C. Andoni Zubizarreta

86. What is the longest period in which the goalkeeper Victor Valdez didn't concede any goals?
    A. 710 minutes
    B. 794 minutes
    C. 896 minutes

87. Which goalkeeper marked the longest period without conceding a goal in La Liga?
    A. Claudio Bravo
    B. Miguel Reina
    C. Victor Valdes

88. Which goal keeper made the most clean-sheets in a season?
    A. Claudio Bravo
    B. Miguel Reina
    C. Victor Valdes

89. Who is considered the most successful president of the club?
    A. Raimon Carrasco
    B. Joan Laporta
    C. Enric Reyna

90. Who is the current president of the club?
    A. Josep Maria Bartomeu
    B. Josep Lluis Nunez
    C. Sandro Rosell

Here are the answers to the last set of questions.

A81. The biggest win in any competition for Barcelona is 18-0 against Taragona as a part of Copa Macaya Championship in 1901.

A82. During the 2015-16 season Barcelona had a run of being unbeaten in 39 consecutive games.

A83. In the 2014-15 season Barcelona marked 50 victories out of 60 possible games in just one season. It was one of the most successful seasons in the club's history as they clinched the Treble by winning La Liga, Copa del Rey and the Champions League.

A84. Barcelona marked the 2011-12 season with a total of 190 goals in all competitions.

A85. Antoni Ramallets Simon spent most of his career at FC Barcelona during the 1950s and early 1960s, winning the Zamora Trophy as the best goalkeeper in La Liga on five occasions.

A86. Víctor Valdes went 896 minutes without conceding a goal in all competitions in the 2011–12 season (from the 22nd minute of the 5th game to the 20th minute of the 12th game). Six games of the Spanish League and three Champions League games were played without conceding a goal.

A87. Miguel Reina went 824 minutes without conceding a goal in the Spanish League in the 1972–73 season. (from the 53rd minute of the 14th game to the 67th minute of the 23rd game).

A88. Víctor Valdes played 535 official games of which he maintained a clean sheet in 237 games, or 44.3% of the matches. The former record was held by Andoni Zubizarreta who played 410 official games of which he maintained a clean sheet in 173 games, or 42.2% of the matches.

A89. Joan Laporta was the most successful president in terms of trophies. In the period from the 15th June 2003 until 30th June 2010 Barcelona won 4 La Ligas, 1 Copa del Reys, 2 Spanish Super Cups, 2 Champions Leagues, 1 UEFA Super Cup and 1 FIFA Club World Cup under his management.

A90. Starting from the 23rd January 2014, the President of FC Barcelona is Josep Maria Bartomeu – fulfilling the position after the resignation of former President, Sandro Rosell.

Here is the final set of questions. Enjoy!

91. What is the nickname of a recent strike force?
    A. AGP
    B. LMN
    C. MSN

92. Who is the city rival of FC Barcelona?
    A. Espanyol
    B. Getafe
    C. Levante

93. What is the name given to any match between fierce rivals Barcelona and Real Madrid?
    A. El Clasico
    B. El Derbi Madrileno
    C. Derby della Madonnina

94. Which Barcelona player has scored the most goals in El Clasico matches?
    A. Pep Guardiola
    B. Andres Iniesta
    C. Lionel Messi

95. Who holds the record for most goals scored in a calendar year?
    A. Johan Cruyff
    B. Diego Maradona
    C. Lionel Messi

96. Which Barcelona player scored the fastest hat-trick?
    A. Pep Guardiola
    B. Andres Iniesta
    C. Pedro Rodriguez

97. How many players have played for both of Spain's biggest football clubs – Barcelona and Real Madrid?
    A. 10
    B. 12
    C. 14

98. How many players have won the European Golden Shoe award whilst at the club?
    A. 2
    B. 3
    C. 4

99. What is the club's official website address?
    A. fcbarcelona.es
    B. fcbarcelona.com
    C. barça.com

100.   What is the club's official twitter account?
    A. @FCBarcelona
    B. @FCBarça
    C. @BarcelonaOfficial

101.   Which of the following is the club anthem?
    A. El Cant del Barça

B. Himno del Barcelona
C. Hola Barça

Here are the answers to the last set of questions.

A91. Lionel Messi, Luis Suarez and Neymar were the fantastic trio that was known as "MSN". Messi, Suarez and Neymar scored a staggering 270 goals between them during their short time together at the club.

A92. The city rival of FC Barcelona is RCD Espanyol since both clubs are located in the Barcelona metropolitan area.

A93. El Clasico is the name given to any match between FC Barcelona and Real Madrid CF. Originally it referred only to those competitions held in the Spanish championship, but nowadays the term has been generalized, and tends to include every single match between the two clubs: Champions League, Copa del Rey, etc. Other than the Champions League Final, it is considered one of the biggest club football games in the world, and is among the most viewed sporting events.

A94. In total, Messi has scored 26 goals against Real Madrid – well ahead of Los Blancos legend Alfredo di Stéfano who scored 18 goals against Barcelona.

A95. Lionel Messi is actually the carrier of Guinness World Record in most goals scored in one calendar year. The astonishing number of goals that Messi scored in one year is 91.

A96. Pedro scored the fastest hat-trick in the club's history in just 9 minutes (34th, 41st and 43rd minutes) in a La Liga game at Getafe on 22nd December 2013.

A97. Ten players have played for both Barcelona and Real Madrid. Those players are Luis Figo, Bernd Schuster, Ronaldo Luís Nazário de Lima, Julen Lopetegui, Robert Prosicencki, Javier Saviola, Gheorghe Hagi, Samuel Eto'o, Luis Enrique and Michael Laudrup.

A98. The European Golden Shoe, formerly European Golden Boot, is awarded to the leading goal scorer in league matches in the top division of every European national league. A total of three players have won the European Golden Shoe while playing for FC Barcelona: Ronaldinho (1996-97), Luis Suarez (2015-16) while Lionel Messi has won the European Golden Shoe 5 times. Messi is the only player to win Ballon d'Or, FIFA World Player of the Year, Pichichi Trophy and European Golden Shoe in the same season

A99. fcbarcelona.com is the official website address.

A100. @FCBarcelona is the official twitter account of the club. It tweets multiple times daily about news at the club, and has over 30 million followers.

A101. By tradition at the Camp Nou, the club anthem, called 'El Cant del Barça' is played on the stadium loudspeaker system, with the fans singing along in unison.

That's it. That's a great question to finish with. I hope you enjoyed this book, and I hope you got most of the answers right.

I also hope you learnt some new facts about the club, and if you spotted anything wrong, or have a general comment, please visit the glowwormpress.com website and send us a message.

Thanks for reading, and if you did enjoy the book, would you please leave a positive review on Amazon.

Made in the USA
Middletown, DE
03 December 2019